GET ▼RICH SLOWLY

...but Surely!

◄●►

Randy L. Thurman, CFP, MBA

GET ▼RICH SLOWLY

...but Surely!

Randy L. Thurman, CFP, MBA

TimeLee™
BOOKS

STARBURST PUBLISHERS™

P.O. Box 4123, Lancaster, Pennsylvania 17604

To schedule Author appearances write:
Author Appearances, Starburst Promotions, P.O. Box 4123,
Lancaster, PA 17604 or call (717)-293-0939.

Randy L. Thurman has now earned the CPA designation.

Credits:

Cover art by Dave Ivey

GET RICH SLOWLY. . . BUT SURELY!

First Printing, April 1992

ISBN: 0-914984-36-5
Library of Congress Catalog Number 91-75193

Printed in the United States of America

**To
Pati,
*My wife and my life.***

Contents

Preface

Why I wrote this book . . .

Ms. H. was having a hard time understanding the principles of *getting rich slowly . . . but surely.* Although she was a young, successful professional, bound and determined to become financially independent—she couldn't understand. "Wouldn't it be OK just to save up in a savings account or money market?" she asked. This was an important question. The answer to which would probably be the difference between her financial independence or dependence at retirement. A difference at retirement of two to thirteen fold. So I started to explain the magic of compound interest, the power of tax-deferral, the power of diversification, the benefit of IRAs, dollar cost averaging, mutual funds and variable annuities. All this within a short amount of allotted time. It really was an impossible task. This was a semester's worth of material crammed into one hour. Although very intelligent, this was not her area of expertise. What could I do? I thought, "Why isn't there a book that could explain these concepts? Explain them in an easy-to-read format so that people who were serious about becoming financially independent could read and re-read at their own pace and level." I sat down and started writing . . . .

Foreword

A hare jeered at a tortoise for the slowness of his pace.

"How do you get anything done?" the hare said.

The tortoise responded, "Well, I always thought you should plan first and then . . ."

"Plan??? No time for that. No time at all," the hare quickly blurted. "What you need is some good exercise."

"Exercise?? Do you mean a . . ." the tortoise began.

"A race, a race," the hare said. Before the tortoise could respond the race was set, the course laid out, and race day came.

At the start the hare was off like a shot and was soon out of the sight of the slow-moving tortoise. Being so far ahead he decided to take a nap by the side of the path.

Meanwhile the tortoise, keeping his goal in mind, kept making steady progress. He thought about taking shortcuts down the rocky hillside, but stuck to the main path and his well-laid plan. Eventually, not even knowing it, he passed the hare, lying in the grass.

It wasn't long before the tortoise crossed the finish line. The hare woke up and ran towards the finish line just in time to see the tortoise crossing it. The moral of the story is . . .

Slow But Steady Wins The Race.

1

The Search For
Financial Independence

Many years ago there was a pleasant young man named Dave, who wanted to become financially independent. Dave wanted the security and independence that came with wealth. His search had led him far and wide over a period of many years.

He read hundreds of investment books, usually titled something like "Get Rich Quick and Easy, in Your Spare Time!" and always grew excited by all the exclamation marks. He paged through the sections on chain letters, raw land, flower bonds, gold coins, multi-level marketing schemes and foreign currency.

He also saw the full spectrum of investment opportunities. Still, he was unhappy.

GET RICH SLOWLY. . .but Surely!

He had seen get-rich-quick schemes that offered a high return with an equally high risk. He even tried more than a few, but they never worked. He found out that if something in the investment world was too good to be true, it usually was. It was an expensive education.

Dave also met with many safe investors. They only invested in CDs or Treasury Bills. Although they received a guaranteed rate of return, Dave wondered how well they were really doing after taxes and inflation. It appeared to him that these investors were not gaining financially. They had the dollars (which he concluded was better than not having any), but their standard of living would eventually decrease because of inflation.

The safe investors would proudly say they had done well.

Yet, he felt uneasy.

It appeared most investors were interested only in returns or only in safety. Dave reasoned that each of these investment strategies was incomplete. It was like taking a drive to a nearby town. You could drive at 120 mph or 10 mph. Neither really seemed appropriate.

He flew home exhausted and depressed.

He would have quit his pursuit many years ago, but he had one thing going for him. He knew precisely what he wanted. A good investment strategy, he reasoned, is one that considers both safety and return. One that considers the individ-

The Search For Financial Independence

ual's goals. A strategy organized to meet goals in the most reasonable manner.

Dave searched everywhere. He wanted to be financially independent at retirement. However, he only found a few effective investors who were financially independent, but they would not share their secrets. He began to wonder if he would ever find out how to become financially independent. The thought of having to rely on social security or relatives worried him greatly and kept him motivated.

2

An Elderly Gentleman Gives Advice

Then he began hearing wonderful reports about an elderly man named Nelson Rockman, whose place of business was a few miles away. The semi-retired man practiced financial planning for the joy of it and to help others become financially independent. Dave had heard people liked Mr. Rockman because he listened to their goals and objectives. He then would map out an organized plan to assist them in becoming financially independent. He used proven investment techniques and philosophies that have withstood the test of time. Dave questioned whether the reports were true, and even if they were, would this man share his secrets?

Dave's desire for answers made him telephone Mr. Rockman's receptionist for an appointment. The receptionist put him through at once.

Dave asked for an appointment. "Sure, how about Tuesday at 2:00 PM or Friday at noon?"

GET RICH SLOWLY. . . but Surely!

The appointment was set for Friday. Dave wondered . . . could this be the person?

When Dave reached the office he found Mr. Rockman staring at a plaque on the wall. "Hello," said Dave. Mr. Rockman turned and smiled. He asked Dave to sit and inquired, "What may I do for you?"

Dave replied, "I'd be grateful if I could ask some questions about how you help people become financially independent."

The elderly gentleman said, "Fire away."

"Please tell me," Dave began, "what is your investment philosophy?"

Mr. Rockman looked into Dave's eyes to see if he was serious. Dave was very serious. He began by saying, "First, financial independence, much like success, is a journey not a destination. I believe an individual should go through a process like this one:

1. *Know where you are.*
2. *Know where you want to be. Set goals. Be specific (e.g., time, amount, etc.)*
3. *Know and plan how to get there.*
4. *ACT!*
5. *Review, review, review.*

An Elderly Gentleman Gives Advice

Let's look at each of these a little bit closer.

Step one—*Know where you are.*

This involves some paperwork. First, prepare a net worth statement. This is where you add up everything you own, subtract everything you owe, and that is your net worth. Then, check this each year to see how you're doing.

Second, prepare an income and expense statement. This is what you bring home and where it goes. Usually this is an enlightening experience for most people.

Step two—*Know where you want to be.*

This is basically goal setting. Goal setting has the same fundamentals regardless of the area (financial, professional, family, social, spiritual). These fundamentals must be accomplished otherwise your goals are only dreams that will vanish into thin air. Goals must be believable, realistic, ardently desired, clearly defined, and most importantly, in writing.

Step three—*Know and plan how to get there.*

Develop a road map to financial independence. How much of your present income can go to your future. Look at your expenses. What expenses can be reduced? Look again. Where do you want to be in one, five, ten, twenty years? If you don't plan and set goals, how do you know when you get there?

GET RICH SLOWLY. . . but Surely!

Step four—*Act!*

The best plan in the world is useless unless you act.

Step five—*Review, review, review.*

At least once a year look at how you're doing. Are you ahead or behind your plan? Have the tax laws changed? Has your situation changed? It is usually best to pick a day in the year to review, maybe January 1 or a birthday.

The individual then should structure that process around a sound investment philosophy like this one:

FIXED ASSETS	EQUITY ASSETS
Examples: Corporate Bonds Long-Term CDs Municipal Bonds Treasury Bonds	*Examples:* Stocks Mutual Funds Real Estate Home Ownership Variable Annuities
CASH RESERVES	**RISK MANAGEMENT**
Examples: Money Market Savings Account Checking Account T-Bills	*Examples:* Life Insurance Health Insurance Disability Insurance Home Owners Insurance

An Elderly Gentleman Gives Advice

First, build your financial foundation with *cash reserves* and *risk management*. You need about 3 months of your monthly expenses set aside for emergency purposes. Examples of cash reserves are savings accounts, money markets, T-bills and short term (less than 1 year) CDs. The risk management area is to cover the things you can't afford to lose. For example: your ability to earn income, your house, your car, etc. Many times you can transfer these risks through insurance. After considering those two areas, cash reserves and risk management, you then start investing for goals like retirement and children's education. And always analyze ways to reduce and defer taxes. Am I telling you more than you want to know?"

"No," Dave said. He had just learned more in two minutes than he had in studying all this time. "I'm looking to become financially independent. To be in the position, say at age 65, to work only because I want to, not because I have to."

"It's good that you have those goals. You will, however, have to plan ahead and work your plan. It's absurd that most people spend more time planning their vacation than they do their financial future. I guess that's why it didn't surprise me when the social security administration said that 87% of the people age 65 years and older are living on less than $10,000 per year. EIGHTY-SEVEN PERCENT. It's a scary thought. Do you have your cash reserves and risk management areas in place?"

GET RICH SLOWLY. . . but Surely!

"Yes, I feel very comfortable with those areas."

"Great! Frankly, the best way to become financially independent is to follow a few simple secrets and powers. If you know and understand these principles, financial independence is not a matter of chance, it's a matter of choice. Most people make financial decisions using two emotions, greed or fear. Greed tries to get rich quick and fails; fear tries to go broke safely and succeeds."

Dave glanced at the plaque on the wall that Mr. Rockman had been staring at earlier. It read:

An Elderly Gentleman Gives Advice

Remember, that time is money. . .
the way to wealth, if you desire it,
is to waste neither time nor money,
but make the best use of both.

Ben Franklin

3

Ten Words or Less

Dave started, "If you could describe your philosophy in ten words or less, what would it be?"

"That's easy," said Rockman, "I believe in getting rich slowly . . . but surely."

Dave's expression was one of amazement and doubt. "Get rich slowly . . . but surely?" he repeated.

Rockman saw this and said, "I use that phrase because a sound investment philosophy performs well over time. One that works long term—say over 10 years."

Though Dave had visited with dozens of investors and read hundreds of books, he had never found anything like this. It was tough to accept. Get rich slowly . . . but surely? Someone who gets good returns without being too risky?

GET RICH SLOWLY. . .but Surely!

The doubt on Dave's face bothered Rockman. "You don't believe, do you? You don't believe in getting rich slowly . . . but surely?"

"It's tough for me to grasp," admitted Dave.

Rockman again chuckled and said, "I understand how you feel. I once felt that way myself. You should visit with some of my colleagues and clients. If you do, I know you'll discover the secrets of getting rich slowly . . . but surely. With this knowledge you'll be on your way to becoming financially independent."

Rockman walked over to the window and stared outside his office. He said, "The average American has one of the lowest savings rates in the developed world. Why?"

"Well," Dave said, "because we are a buy now, pay later society. The money decisions that lead to financial independence must compete with consumerism."

"That's right!" the older man shouted, "most people's expenses rise to meet their income. We call it *Parkinson's Eighth Law*. Or to put it another way, most people have too much month at the end of their money. People believe they don't have extra income to invest for their future. The present is tough enough. Still, no matter what your income, you can find money to save. It's simply a matter of repositioning your priorities and discipline."

Mr. Rockman pulled out a list of names from his desk and handed it to Dave.

Ten Words or Less

"These are the names and phone numbers of six people who are either clients or colleagues," Mr. Rockman explained, "I would suggest you speak to as many of them as you can."

Then Rockman looked in Dave's eyes and said, "You're searching for financial independence and I admire that," he stood up and shook Dave's hand.

"After talking with my clients and colleagues, if you have any questions," he said sincerely, "come back to see me. I understand your need to learn how to become financially independent. I would like to give you the underlying principles. Many years ago, someone gave them to me. It is my hope that you fully understand them. If you apply these principles, you will become financially independent."

"Thanks."

As he left the office, partially stunned, he walked by the secretary who said empathetically, "Maybe I can be of some help. I've phoned all the people on the list. Five are available and have agreed to share the secrets of the 'getting rich slowly . . . but surely' philosophy with you."

Dave thanked her and decided to visit all five: Mr. Duncan, Ms. Lindsay, Mr. Bollinger, Ms. McNeil and Mr. Hartman.

4

Five Roadblocks to Success

Dave met Mr. Duncan at his office. Duncan greeted him with a big smile and said, "So I hear you've seen the ol' man. He's a unique individual isn't he?"

"Yes he is," Dave responded, thinking that "unique" could be good or bad.

"Did he tell you about getting rich slowly . . . but surely?"

"Yes he did. It isn't true, is it?"

"It sure is. I owe my financial independence to the underlying principles. These principles involve the knowledge of investment risks and the secrets and powers to overcome them.

Actually, there are five major risks or roadblocks that keep people from achieving their financial goals. They are:

GET RICH SLOWLY. . .but Surely!

> 1. *Procrastination*
> 2. *Business risk*
> 3. *Purchasing power risk*
> 4. *Taxes*
> 5. *Volatility risk*

As there are five risks and roadblocks, there are five secrets or powers to overcome them. I'll be sharing with you the *procrastination* roadblock and the *power of compound interest*.

The number one reason people fail financially is *procrastination. Procrastination* is the thief of time. There will never be a good time to get started. Too many people let the following be the story of their life:

Age 21-30—*I can't invest now.*

There's plenty of time. I'm young and don't make a lot yet. I'll wait till I start making more then I'll start investing.

Age 30-45—*I can't invest now.*

It takes all I make with a growing family on my hands. Between them and my house payments it takes all I have. When they're older, it will cost less. Then I'll start saving.

Five Roadblocks to Success

Age 45-55—*I can't invest now.*

My kids are in college. It's all I can do to manage to pay their expenses. I'll wait until they get out of college then I'll really start investing.

Age 55-65—*I can't save now.*

I know I should, but things aren't breaking like they were when I was younger. It's difficult for a person my age to find a better paying job. I guess I'll ride along and see what happens and hope for the best.

I wish I would have started earlier.

It's a sad story but unfortunately too often true. If they only had known about the *power of compound interest*. If they had, they would have known you don't have to save a lot to become financially independent. It really takes two things: time and discipline."

"Tell me, what is the *power of compound interest?*"

"I'm glad you asked," Duncan said, "Compound interest uses time to your advantage. Let's look at these four people.

Person 1

A 26-year-old makes a $2000 annual IRA contribution on his birthday. He continues to make that contribution for nine more years. The total contributions equal $20,000.

GET RICH SLOWLY. . .but Surely!

Person 2

A 35-year-old makes a $3000 annual contribution to his retirement plan. He continues to make those contributions until he retires at the age of 65. The total contributions equal $93,000.

Person 3

A 45-year-old makes a $10,000 annual contribution to his retirement plan. He continues to make those contributions until he retires at age 65. The total contributions equal $220,000.

Person 4

A 55-year-old makes a $40,000 annual contribution to his retirement plan (if that were possible). He continues until he retires at age 65. The contributions equal $440,000.

Assuming a fixed rate of return of twelve percent, which person would retire at age 65 a millionaire?"

"Sounds like a trick question," Dave responded, "I would guess person **4** because he put in almost a half million to work with."

"It is a trick question," Duncan said with a big grin, "Person number **4** will have $826,183. Persons number **2** and **3** will have $813,877 and $816,987 respectively. Person number **1** is our millionaire with $1,051,517 though he put in the least money. The reason is the *power of compound interest*. The only way to have the *power of compound interest* work for you is by defeating procrastination."

Dave remembered the plaque on Mr. Rockman's wall. He also noticed two similar plaques on Duncan's wall, they read:

He that waits on a fortune
is never sure of dinner.

and

No great thing is created suddenly,
anymore than a bunch
of grapes or a fig.
If you tell me that you desire a fig,
I answer you that there
must be time.
Let it blossom, then bear fruit,
then ripen.

Epictetus (AD 55-135)

5

Investment Return Rates

"Please go on," Dave prodded as he pulled out his pad and pencil.

Duncan continued, "For example, I used to think that investment return rates were simple to understand. If you invested $100 say at a rate of 6% you would have X in 10 years. And if you invested $100 at 12%, since 12% is twice 6% you would have X times 2. This seems fairly simple and straightforward. It is so straightforward that it is wrong. Then someone showed me a compound interest table like this one:"

The Power of Compound Interest
$100/month

LENGTH OF INVESTMENT

	10 Years	*20 Years*	*30 Years*	*40 Years*
Return				
6%	16,470	46,435	100,954	200,144
10%	20,655	76,570	227,933	637,678
12%	23,234	99,915	352,991	1,188,242
15%	27,866	151,595	700,982	3,140,376

GET RICH SLOWLY. . .but Surely!

"That's when I discovered that the amount I invest, although important, is not nearly as important as time and the rate of return. It is amazing how a few extra percentage points can make so much difference down the road.

I then found the *power of compound interest* worked the same way for lump sum or monthly investing. I really didn't know why it worked, but a graph helped somewhat," Duncan said. He pulled out a file and showed Dave the following graphs.

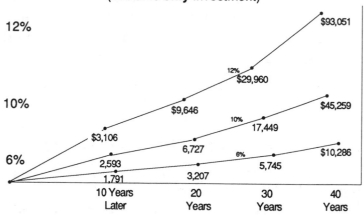

**THE POWER OF COMPOUND INTEREST
LUMP SUM OF $1,000**
(one time **only** investment)

Investment Return Rates

THE POWER OF COMPOUND INTEREST
$100/MONTH
$100/Month (put in at first of month)

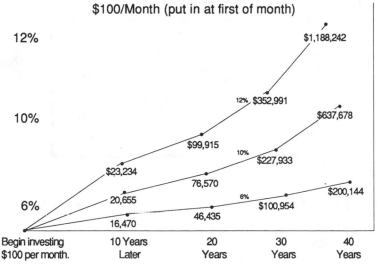

"The *power of compound interest* has a secret rule also. It's called the rule of 72. The rule of 72 has been extremely valuable to me as an investor but they never taught me this in business school. This secret answers the question, how long will it take my money to double? Or, how long will it take my $100 to become $200 at various rates of return. The rule is simply 72 divided by the interest rate equals the number of years to double. Here is an example."

GET RICH SLOWLY. . .but Surely!

Rule Of 72			
72 /	Interest Rate	=	Years
72	3%		24
72	6%		12
72	9%		8
72	12%		6
72	15%		4.8

Dave thought for a while, then became uneasy. Certainly, he wanted a higher return, but his past experience revealed there would be trade-offs. He was afraid of risks. "What about the risks?" he asked.

"Good question. One I'd hope you'd ask. There are three major types of risk: business risk, purchasing power risk, and volatility risk. All investments have various degrees of risk. There is no such thing as a totally safe investment. You will soon discover ways to reduce or almost eliminate them in the long run," the man replied.

"Sounds interesting. I'm all for reducing risk, but what is business risk?"

Mr. Duncan smiled, looked at his watch and said, "Why don't you ask Ms. Lindsay. She's on your list, isn't she?"

Dave was impressed. "How did Mr. Duncan know that?" Dave felt that maybe he wasn't the first to

Investment Return Rates

go through this *pony express* education. "Yes, she is." He rose to shake Duncan's hand. "Thanks so much for your time, sir."

"You're welcome," Duncan responded, "since I've become financially independent, I have more time to do the things I want."

Dave left Duncan's office, thinking about the simplicity of it all. He thought it certainly made sense. Use time and return to your advantage. He wondered if the other secrets and powers would be so easy.

6

Business Risk

He drove to his next appointment. When he arrived at Ms. Lindsay's office he was surprised to see such a young woman. Ms. Lindsay was in her early 30's, and impeccably dressed.

"So you've been to see the ol' man. He's a unique individual, isn't he?" Ms. Lindsay said.

Again, Dave really didn't know how to take that, but he was not surprised at Mr. Rockman being called a unique individual.

"Yes, he is," said Dave.

"So, did he share with you about getting rich slowly . . . but surely?" she asked.

"He certainly did. It isn't true is it?" asked Dave, testing to see whether he would get a different response.

GET RICH SLOWLY. . . but Surely!

"Rest assured, it's true. I'm well on my way to becoming financially independent," she replied.

"How are you doing that?"

"Essentially, through the principles of getting rich slowly . . . but surely. These principles overcome the risks and roadblocks of investing by using the secrets and powers of the philosophy," she replied.

"Yes, I know about the power of *compound interest* and the *procrastination* roadblock," interrupted Dave.

Lindsay said, "That's great, but I wasn't thinking about the roadblock of *procrastination*. I was thinking about *business risk* and the *power of diversification*."

"What is *business risk?* How did you find out about it?"

Lindsay began, "I was like everyone else, wanting a big return without any risks—risks of losing my dollars that is. Unfortunately, it's not that simple. I searched and tried those get-rich-quick schemes. They never worked. Hot stock tips from my dentist also never worked. I found out the hard way. There are two times when you shouldn't try to get-rich-quick: when you can afford it and when you can't."

"Do you still get advice from your dentist?" asked Dave sarcastically.

"Yes, but only for dental work. I get my investment advice from professional investment advisors, like the ol'man. He showed me the secrets and powers

42

Business Risk

that reduced my risks and increased my return in the long run. My objective is to be financially independent at retirement. I was looking for strategies that, while not hitting a home run, would hit several singles. Something that would give me a good long run return and let me sleep at night. Most people try to hit the big home run by buying low and selling high or they try to put all their eggs in one basket. Buy low, sell high, sounds great in theory; but it can rarely be done. Predicting the future is impossible. The only sensible strategy for all but the most avid risk avoiders is the *power of diversification*. You know eggs . . . basket . . . that sort of thing.

Most people do the opposite. They put all their eggs in one basket and then try to watch that basket. A very risky move when you're walking on the slippery and shifting road of investments.

7

The Power of Diversification

Let's look at the *power of diversification*. Let's say you had $100,000 to invest and you needed the money in 25 years. You have two choices. The "safe" choice is a guaranteed investment earning 8%. The diversified choice is splitting your $100,000 into five $20,000 investments."

"Pretend that you could read the future and your five investments in the diversified choice looked like this:

Investments	Results
A	You lose everything including your $20,000.
B	You earned 0% on your money.
C	You earned 5% per year on your money.
D	You earned 10% per year on your money.
E	You earned 15% per year on your money.

GET RICH SLOWLY. . . but Surely!

Which one would you choose?"
Dave thought a long time. This also sounded like a trick question. He still had to say, "The 'safe' choice."

"That's what most people would say. That's why most people depend on relatives or social security at retirement," she said firmly. "Let's look again at the diversified choice again. With investment **A** you lost all your money. You didn't apply the principles you will learn. It probably was a hot stock tip. With investment **B** you broke even and had no return at all. Maybe you buried your money. With investment **C** you earned less than the average savings account. Even with these three setbacks, because of the *power of diversification*, you still would have had more than the so called 'safe' choice. Here's why."

The "safe" choice at 8% × 25 = $684,850

The diversified choice:

Return	Investment	Amount
All loss	A	$ 0
0%	B	$ 20,000
5%	C	$ 67,730
10%	D	$ 216,690
15%	E	$ 685,380
	Total	$ 962,800

The Power of Diversification

"The following graphic may help."

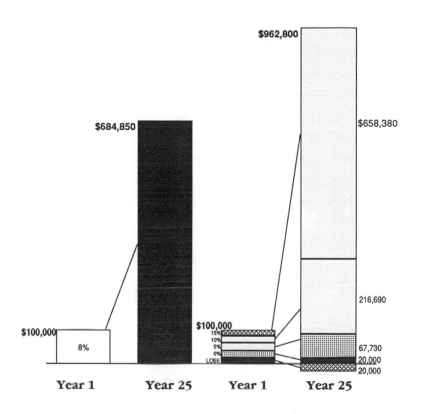

"You may not have $100,000 to invest now, but if you follow the principles you will. Even if you are just starting out with a few dollars a month or a small lump sum, diversification works the same. You actually earned forty percent more just by using the *power of diversification*. You should, however, diversify into more than just five investments. There are ways to diversify into hundreds."

"How can I do that?"

"There are many ways," Lindsay said, "One of which is a mutual fund. A mutual fund is where thousands of people pool their investment dollars and let professionals select, manage, and sell securities on the behalf of the group. Investments in a mutual fund may be acquired in a lump sum or in modest amounts at scheduled intervals. There are many advantages to mutual funds, some of which are:

1. Professional selection of investments.
2. The *power of diversification* (many funds will hold over hundreds of investments).
3. Continuous management and review.

The *power of diversification* adds to your security. Especially if you ask yourself the question, 'Does *security* mean the dollars I have? Or the purchasing power I have?' "

"Well," said Dave, "I would hope both." His mind wandered for a second as he looked upon the wall. He saw two plaques that read:

The Power of Diversification

He that hesitates is not only lost,
but miles away from the next exit.

and

When walking through a melon patch,
don't adjust your sandals.

8

100,000
German Mark

Dave thought about the last plaque and wondered what it had to do with investing. Ms. Lindsay interrupted his train of thought.

"It would be nice in the real world if we could have more dollars and more purchasing power," Lindsay responded. "In the real world, however, inflation or decline of purchasing power of the dollar caused by inflation is a major risk. It's the *Robin Hood* of the nineties. It takes from the ignorant and gives to the well-informed. Most people don't consider purchasing power risk. That's a shame. Over the last twenty years inflation has averaged 6%. At 6%, to maintain your standard of living your income needs to double every. . ."

"Twelve years," Dave interrupted using the rule of 72.

"That's right," Lindsay confirmed, "just ask Mr. Bollinger."

Off he went to see Mr. Bollinger.

———————

Dave knocked on the door.

A tall (6 ft. 5 in.), grey-haired gentleman with a German accent, Mr. Bollinger, answered, "Yes, what is it?" he echoed.

"Mr. Bollinger, my name is Dave. Would you tell me about the biggest risk in investing—*purchasing power risk?*" Dave managed.

"Come in," Bollinger said as his great hand engulfed Dave's.

"So you want to know about *purchasing power risk*, do you?" the gentleman asked. "You must have visited with the young man down the road."

"Yes, sir," covering up a chuckle at the thought of the elderly gentleman being called a young man. "Age is a relative thing," he thought. But with this giant of a man, Dave felt a stronger need to be as polite as possible.

"Well, I know about inflation—first hand. I lived in Germany in 1923," Bollinger said.

Dave quickly calculated the rough age of Mr. Bollinger, and was amazed. He didn't look a day over 55.

Mr. Bollinger stood up, walked over to the

100,000 German Mark

Mr. Bollinger stood up, walked over to the bookshelf, and pulled out a book. Between two pages he pulled out a 4″ x 8″ sheet of purplish paper. He touched it with pride. "This," he boasted, "is a 100,000 German Mark dated February, 1923. This small piece of paper has reminded me of the worst risk of them all, inflation or purchasing power risk. It is like a thief in the night. You never see it taking from you. You don't even notice until it's too late.

This Mark could have purchased the finest Mercedes when it was first printed, and I wish I would have purchased one. Between February and July of that year we had an unbelievable inflation rate. By the end of that year, the Mark wouldn't even buy a loaf of bread. In fact, at the end of the year it was more useful as scratch paper than it was as money. I keep it around to remind me that it's not how much money or dollars you have, but the pounds of food, pairs of shoes, etc. that those dollars will buy that counts. Here in America, people are afraid of losing their money because of the *Great Depression*. In Germany, however, older Germans fear losing purchasing power because of the great inflation. There is much to be said about both."

As Dave was taking in what Mr. Bollinger had said, he noticed two plaques on the wall that read:

*If I had known
that I was going to live this long,
I would have taken
better care of myself.*

and

*The reason it is so difficult
to make ends meet
is because someone is
always moving the ends.*

9

Return vs. Inflation

"The return you should seek," Mr. Bollinger continued, "is the real rate of return. For example, if you are getting 6% return and inflation is at 6% what is your real rate of return?"

"Well, I want to say it is 6%, but that's not right is it?" Dave was getting used to trick questions.

"No, it's not, young man. If you're getting a 6% return and inflation is running at 6% you're only breaking even. Real rate of return is calculated like this:

Return 6% – Inflation 6% = Real Rate 0%

So you see, your focus should be the real rate of return. And this example doesn't even consider taxes."

"Which is one of the two great certainties of life," Dave added.

GET RICH SLOWLY. . .but Surely!

The gentleman grinned and laughed, "Yes, that's true. Death and taxes are life's two great certainties. Yet, death only happens once and doesn't get worse every time Congress meets."

Now it was Dave's turn to laugh. "That sounds great, but I don't like my investment to go down in value. It makes me nervous."

"I understand what you mean. The investments that keep pace with inflation, do tend to fluctuate. There are techniques that can help you reduce this risk of volatility. One is to *diversify*. When one investment is going down, the other hopefully is going up. The more you diversify the more you spread the volatility of wild swings in your investments to a minimum. Diversification reduces volatility, but does not eliminate it. The second is a method that will take advantage of those same fluctuations when they do occur. It's called *dollar cost averaging*. This technique allows you to reduce your risk and increase your potential return. And that's all you can ask from an investment strategy, isn't it?"

"Yes, please tell me about this strategy that can reduce my risk and increase my potential return," asked Dave excitedly. "Is that possible?"

"Not in the short term, but it is almost certain in the long run. But Ms. McNeil could better answer that for you. Why don't you ask her?" Mr. Bollinger suggested.

10

Dollar Cost Averaging

The next morning Dave walked into Ms. McNeil's office. She asked how she could help him. After several minutes of discussion about financial independence, Dave remarked, "Do you have any suggestions?"

"Well," Ms. McNeil began, "because you are wanting to get rich slowly... but surely, I would suggest an investment strategy that would reduce your risk and increase your potential long-term return. Does that sound like what you're looking for?"

"Why yes," Dave replied.

"One of the best time-tested strategies for the long term is called *dollar cost averaging*," she continued. "For example, let's say you invested $100 per year for six years. Your investment looked like this graph:"

GET RICH SLOWLY. . .but Surely!

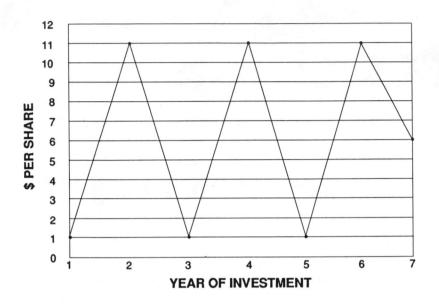

"In the seventh year, you sold at what appears to be at an average price per share of $6 [(11+1)/2]. The power of *dollar cost averaging* works like this:"

Amount Invested	Shares
$300	300 @ $ 1.00
300	27.27 @ $11.00
$600	327.27 shares

Dollar Cost Averaging

"Average cost per share = $600/327.27 = $1.83. An amount much less than average price of $6 per share.

You might also think that you broke even and didn't make any money—since you sold halfway between $11 per share and $1 per share. Still, the power of dollar cost averaging comes through again. If you sell 327.27 shares at $6 per share that would give you $1963.62. Considerable profit for the $600 invested.

Dollar cost averaging can even make you money in a down market. For example, look at these three examples. You invest $1000 annually for six years. Tell me which one do you make the most money on?"

Dave carefully studied the graphic example on page 60.

UNDERSTANDING DOLLAR COST AVERAGING

GET RICH SLOWLY. . .but Surely!

	1985	1986	1987	1988	1989	1990	ACCUMULATED SHARES	LIQUIDATION VALUE
#1	$10	$12	$14	$16	$18	$20	425	$8500
#2	$10	$8	$5	$5	$8	$10	850	$8500
#3	$10	$8	$5	$1	$1	$4	2675	$10,700

INVEST $1,000 EACH OF 6 PURCHASE PERIODS

Dollar Cost Averaging

"Well," replied Dave hesitantly, anticipating a trick question. (He believed #1 to be the obvious choice—because it went straight up. However, because the obvious choice was undoubtedly wrong, he didn't want to answer number one.) "How about number two?"

"No," smiled Ms. McNeil, "the answer is number three! Choices one and two would produce $8,500 while choice number 3 would have grown to $10,700. Almost 21% more. That's the power of *dollar cost averaging*. Now *dollar cost averaging* doesn't guarantee that you'll make money, especially in the short term. But, it does reduce your risk and increase your potential for return in the long-term.

This type of strategy also works best on those investments that move up and down."

"How long is long-term?" questioned Dave.

"Your investment objective needs to be at least 7 to 10 years and preferably 15 years. You may want to know that since 1934, in the mutual fund I use, there has never been a 15 year period where *dollar cost averaging* has lost money. Now, that doesn't guarantee it won't happen in the future, but that's a good track record—42 out of 42. If you had placed $250 initially and added $100 monthly to this investment beginning January 1, 1975 and continued through December 31, 1989, you would have $74,302—over a 15% return. Here again, past performance is not a guarantee of future performance. However, *dollar cost averaging* has been around a long time. It's still around because it works so well.

It works best when you diversify your investment to reduce business risk and use the power of tax deferral."

"Let me guess. I need to see Mr. Hartman the CPA for that?" Dave was getting used to the routine.

"Yes, you'd better ask Mr. Hartman. He'll explain it to you."

On the way out, Dave noticed a plaque on the wall. It read:

Dollar Cost Averaging

Employ thy time well if thou meanest to gain leisure.

11

Tax Deferral

As he sat in the waiting room, Dave noticed that Mr. Hartman's office was small but impressive. A plaque on the wall read:

Over and over again courts have said that there is nothing sinister in so arranging one's affairs as to keep taxes as low as possible. Everybody does so, rich or poor, and all do right. For nobody owes any public duty to pay more than the law demands: taxes are enforced exactions, not voluntary contributions. To demand more in the name of morals is mere cant.

Justice Learned Hand
Commissioner vs Newman
159 F. 2d 848 (2d Cir., 1947)

GET RICH SLOWLY. . .but Surely!

Mr. Hartman greeted Dave with, "So you want to know about the *power of tax deferral* do you?"

"Yes."

"Please, come into my office." As Dave was seated, Mr. Hartman began, "You can learn to cash in on the benefits of before tax dollars and on the *power of tax deferral*. What is tax deferral? Tax deferral is an arrangement where all the earnings, the interest, and dividends accumulate without having to pay tax on them until they are withdrawn. Examples of tax deferred accounts are annuities and qualified retirement plans, such as IRAs. I would first like to show you the advantages of the power of tax deferral and then explain about annuities and IRAs. Would that be OK?"

"Sure."

"The advantages of tax deferral are clear. For every dollar not taken out of your investment earnings to pay taxes, your money will accumulate even faster for you.

And keep in mind that if contributions are tax deductible or before tax dollars, like deductible IRAs and qualified retirement plans at work, you enjoy even greater benefits.

Look at these charts. The first chart looks at a lump sum of $10,000 comparing before tax dollars, tax deferred dollars and after tax dollars.

The second chart is the same comparison except it assumes $167/month investment. Both use a 12% return rate. What a difference!"

Tax Deferral

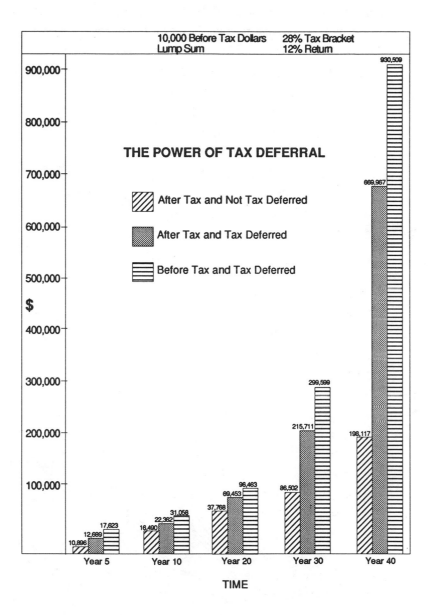

GET RICH SLOWLY. . .but Surely!

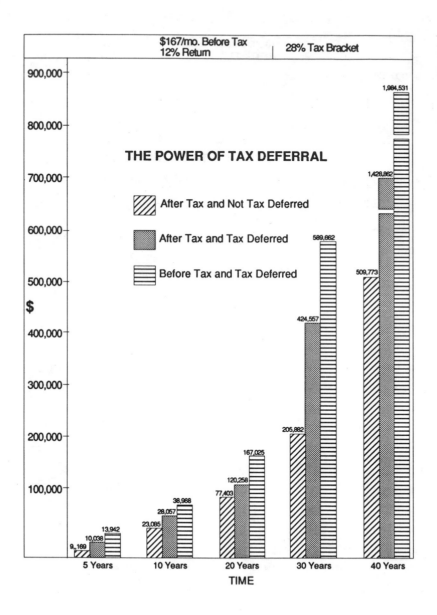

THE POWER OF TAX DEFERRAL

$167/mo. Before Tax 12% Return · 28% Tax Bracket

- After Tax and Not Tax Deferred
- After Tax and Tax Deferred
- Before Tax and Tax Deferred

Tax Deferral

"We assume you pay tax on your taxable investment from year to year. You would pay tax when you draw it out of the tax favored account. By investing $167/month in before tax dollars, in a tax deferred vehicle assuming a 12% return and 28% marginal tax bracket you would accumulate almost 3½ times more than the after tax investment. Yes, you would have to pay taxes when you withdrew money, but even then you would have multiples more than the non-tax advantaged way. That's the *power of tax deferral*."

12

Annuities and IRAs

Dave took a breath and said, "May I ask you some questions?"

"Of course," Hartman replied.

"First, what is an annuity?"

"I'm glad you asked because I was going to go into that. Annuities are investments where your money compounds tax deferred until you take it out. There are two types of annuities, *fixed* and *variable*. A *fixed annuity* gives you a set guaranteed rate of return. A *variable annuity*, on the other hand, directs your funds to be invested in one or a combination of mutual funds. For example, a variable annuity may have the following choices:

GET RICH SLOWLY. . . but Surely!

1. *Money market*
2. *Fixed account*
3. *Corporate Bonds*
4. *Managed Accounts*
5. *Government Securities*
6. *Stock Fund*
7. *Asset Allocation*
8. *International Fund*

You can see there are many choices.

There are also some additional benefits to annuities:

1. All earnings accumulate tax deferred until withdrawn.

2. There generally is not a sales charge or commission taken out up front. 100% of your money goes to work for you.

3. A variable annuity has flexibility. You may change investment options when you want.

4. An annuity can avoid probate if set up properly."

"Thank you," said Dave wide-eyed. "Now please explain what is an *IRA* and what are the new rules that apply."

Annuities and IRAs

"An *IRA* is a personal tax deferred retirement account."

"Who may contribute?"

"Well," said Hartman, "Anyone under the age of 70½ with earned income may contribute up to $2000 or 100% of earned income if less, to an *IRA*. All earnings will be tax deferred, but the contributions will be fully or partially deductible for some taxpayers and not for others."

"How do you know if you can deduct it?"

"This is an area commonly misunderstood. The deductibility depends on two things," Hartman said. "First, whether or not the taxpayer or spouse has the ability to participate in a qualified retirement plan through work, and secondly, how much money they earn. If the taxpayer or spouse does not have access to an employer retirement plan then the *IRA* is automatically deductible, regardless how much money they earn. If a couple has an adjusted gross income of less than $40,000 or an individual has an adjusted gross income of less than $25,000 a full deduction can be taken even if participating in an employer's retirement plan. If you have adjusted gross income between $40,000 and $50,000 for couples ($25,000-$35,000 for individuals) your tax deduction for *IRA* contributions is reduced by $200 for each $1000 of income above $40,000 for couples and $25,000 for individuals. To simplify this, I have a table for you that might help you to understand." He handed Dave the following:

GET RICH SLOWLY. . .but Surely!

Employer Plan Available	Income	Amount Deductable
No	over $2000	$2000
Yes	up to $40,000 ($25,000 for individuals)	$2000
Yes	$40,000-$50,000 ($25,000-$35,000)	$0-$2000 Phased out at rate of $200 for each $1000 of income above established limits.
Yes	over $50,000 ($35,000 for individuals)	$0

Annuities and IRAs

"The tax laws are constantly changing, so you want to check with your tax advisor before making any solid decisions.

In summary, for long term investment goals you want to:

1. Decide how much you want to set aside for long term investing, such as retirement. As a general rule, a minimum of 10% of your income should be set aside.

2. Place these dollars into a before-tax investment if possible.

3. If it is not possible, or if you are at contribution limits, place dollars in a tax deferred investment.

Now to tie it all together—why don't you pay the ol' man another visit?" Hartman suggested.

13

Another Visit to Mr. Rockman

"Now what have you learned?" asked Mr. Rockman as he lowered his head to peer above his bifocals.

"Well," said Dave with enthusiasm, "I've seen how a few percentage points difference in my return can make a vast difference because of the *power of compound interest*. I know that inflation is a hidden thief and I should look at the real rate of return. The *power of diversification* and *dollar cost averaging* allows me to reduce my risk and increase my potential long-term returns. The *power of using before tax dollars* and *tax deferral* can be the difference between being dependent and financially independent."

GET RICH SLOWLY. . . but Surely!

"Great! Would you like to see what these powers mean to you? Let's look at a hypothetical example of two investors. One used the techniques, powers, and secrets that you've learned and one didn't. First, let's look at the one who didn't. We'll call him Buford. Buford has $167 per month to invest. Because he choses to be taxed on that amount and he's in the 28% tax bracket, the $167 per month becomes $120 after taxes to invest [167 x (1 –.28)]. He invests only in "safe" investments, so he puts his money into a *NOW* account at the bank where he will earn 6%. Because the interest is taxed, the after tax equivalent yield is 4.32%. If he had started at your age (35) and accumulated for retirement, he would have $88,643. Not a bad nest egg. But how long do you think it will last with inflated prices?

Yet, had he put the money in a diversified account, before-tax and tax deferred investment that was earning 15%, using dollar cost averaging, he would have $1,170,807. If he had earned 18% he would have $2,392,490.

Truly, these are the secrets of getting rich slowly . . . but surely. A difference of over 13 fold."

Dave left amazed that such simple ideas could yield such a tremendous difference. He wrote out his plan of action and applied the principles; then he stuck by them. Sure, those get-rich-quick schemes tempted him again and again. Those so called "safe" investments also tempted him when

Another Visit to Mr. Rockman

the market dipped down. But he didn't change his sandals in the middle of the watermelon patch and he became rich slowly . . . but surely and financially independent.

14

Share The Secrets!

After many years passed, Dave thought back to this day, smiling and remembering how much he had learned from the elderly gentleman. It seemed like yesterday. Now Dave was as old as Mr. Rockman was back then. But he didn't feel old. He was happy to be financially independent. He decided that he needed to write down these principles in a book. A book of financial independence. A book of getting rich slowly . . . but surely.

After Dave had written his book, he handed copies out to many people. He gave them to everyone who wanted to become financially independent. Having this knowledge written down allowed people to learn at their own pace. If they didn't understand a certain area they could read and reread it until the concept was grasped. Giving his book out to people wanting to learn the secrets made him happy. He remembered a letter that said, "Thank you. Your book has made a positive impact on my life." That pleased him.

Sharing wisdom in this easy way made him very popular.

Everyone knew this was not a get-rich-quick scheme, but one that worked with time and allowed a good rate of return. He stared at the plaque on the wall that reminded him of the secrets that read:

1. *The Tortoise Won*
2. *ACT!*
3. *Eggs . . . Basket . . .*
4. *Germany, 1923*
5. *Dollar Cost Average*
6. *Defer taxes*

It amazed Dave how many people, who had read the book and applied these same principles, became financially independent. These people gave the book to others they knew who also became financially independent. He laughed when he thought of the book gaining popularity like a chain letter (something he had tried in his early, misguided days).

Share The Secrets

As Dave sat at his enormous desk, he realized what a lucky man he was. To have become financially independent without depending on social security, family, or the U.S. government for help. Being financially independent gave him time. Time to do the things he wanted to do. Although he was still working, it was because he wanted to, not because he *had* to. He had time to exercise. Time to spend with his grandchildren. Time to travel and money to do so. He was glad he didn't wait to use the techniques of getting rich slowly . . . but surely. He had watched his children grow up and apply the principles. They too became rich slowly . . . but surely and financially independent.

Dave felt successful as a person, and as an investor. He discovered the biggest reward of his financial planning, besides being financially independent, was to help others find the way. His caring for people and his sharing had paid handsome dividends. He spoke to many organizations and received many community service awards.

His secretary broke his trance when she walked into the room and said, "Excuse me, a young woman on the phone wants to know if she can talk to you about becoming financially independent."

He was glad. He believed everyone should become more involved in financial matters. It appeared that now it was happening.

GET RICH SLOWLY. . .but Surely!

"How about Tuesday at 2:00 PM, or Friday at noon?" he heard himself saying.

It wasn't long until he found himself talking with a bright young woman. He shared the secrets of how to *get rich slowly. . . but surely* and knew she would follow the principles to becoming financially independent.

After telling the young woman his valuable secrets he said, "There is a way for you to pay me back many times over. Will you do just one thing for me?"

"What is that?" she asked.

"Share the secrets."

Glossary

Before Tax Dollars—Taxes have not been applied to those dollars. An example would be tax deductable IRAs.

Business Risk—The risk that you can lose your dollars in an investment. An example would be investing in a stock and the company goes bankrupt. Hence the term business risk.

Buy Low, Sell High—No such thing.

Cash Reserves—Investments that can easily be converted to cash at little or no loss. Examples are savings accounts, money markets, T-bills, cash value life insurance and short-term (less than 1 year) Certificates of Deposits (CDs). The general rule of thumb is to have three to six months of your monthly expenses in cash reserves.

Compound Interest—Interest earned on interest. The effect is like a snowball rolling downhill getting bigger, quicker.

Diversification—Spreading your risks and investments, thereby, reducing or almost eliminating some types of risks (e.g. business risk) through a mutual fund or variable annuity.

GET RICH SLOWLY. . . but Surely!

Dollar Cost Averaging—An investment technique that allows you to reduce your risk and increase your potential return. The technique calls for a set dollar amount invested on a periodic basis.

Financially Independent—To be in a position, financially, that if you're working it's because you want to, not because you have to. In other words, that point in time where retirement is affordable and work is optional.

Fixed Annuity—An investment offered through life insurance companies giving you a fixed rate of return. Your return grows tax-deferred until you take it out. Allows the power of tax-deferral to work for you.

Get-Rich-Quick—See Buy Low, Sell High.

IRA—A tax advantage the IRS allows. It is a personal tax-deferred retirement account. Many times you can use before-tax dollars which reduces your current tax burden. You can invest your IRA dollars in many investments including mutual funds and variable annuities.

Mark—A form of money in Germany. Like the dollar in the U.S.

Mutual Fund—A method of investing where thousands of people pool their investment dollars and let professionals select, buy, manage, and sell securities on behalf of the group. A great way to diversify.

Purchasing Power Risk—Probably the greatest risk of all because it is hidden and mostly unknown. It is the loss of purchasing power because of inflation. At

Glossary

a 6% inflation rate your income needs to double every 12 years just to maintain your standard of living.

Real Rate of Return—Nominal Rate of Return minus inflation.

Risk Management—To analyze the risks of life. Undesireable large risks should be transferred to an insurance company if possible.

Variable Annuity—An investment offered through life insurance companies giving you many choices on where to invest your dollars. Allows you to invest in mutual-fund-like investments, that grow tax-deferred.

Volatility Risk—The risk that the investment will move up and down in value, and in a manner that is unpredictable especially in the short-term.

Acknowledgements

It has been said that no one person writes a book alone. This book is no exception. I would like to thank the following people for their inspiration and input toward a book that will help people overcome the roadblocks to financial success.

My clients
Nancee Little, CFP, CPA
Dr. Loynita Spillmeier
Richard Henderson
Regina McDonald
Elizabeth Sheehan
Amanda Harbeston
Doug Oliver
Joe Ward
Dave Robie
Ray Bauer
Lee McKenzie
Students at OKCCC
Students at UCO

Tim Hough, CPA
Joe Bowie, RFP
Jack Kraettli
Dr. Ken Southerland
Tom Hutter
Dick Mayes, CFP
Roxanna Snodgrass
Danny Stith
Leo Thurman
Mike DeYong, JD
John Reardon
Cecil Caid
Toastmaster's International
Erin VanLaanen, JD

To the above named, my sincere thanks and gratitude. To those not named but who helped, a deep appreciation for your contribution.

To all of you I wish the best of luck and God bless you.

Books & Tapes by Starburst Publishers

(Partial listing—full list available on request)

Get Rich Slowly . . . But Surely! —Randy L. Thurman

The only get-rich-quick guide you'll ever need. Achieving financial independence is important to young and old. Anyone who wants to be financially free will discover the way to financial independence easier by applying these long-term, time-tested principles. This book can be read in one sitting!

(trade paper) ISBN 0914984365 **$7.95**

You Can Eliminate Stress From The I.R.S.

—Fulton N. Dobson

Almost everyone can expect to undergo a tax audit at least once or twice in their lifetime. This book gives common sense actions to take that will make the audit easier to face. Answers questions like: What are my rights as a taxpayer? What can I expect from my tax accountant? How can I prove to the IRS my ability (or inability) to pay back taxes? . . . and much more.

(trade paper) ISBN 0914984403 **$7.95**

Like A Bulging Wall —Robert Borrud

Will you survive the 1990's economic crash? This book shows how debt, greed, and covetousness, along with a lifestyle beyond our means, has brought about an explosive situation in this country. Gives "call" from God to prepare for judgement in America, Also lists TOP-RATED U.S. BANKS and SAVINGS & LOANS.

(trade paper) ISBN 0914984284 **$8.95**

What To Do When The Bill Collector Calls!
Know Your Rights —David L. Kelcher, Jr.

Reveals the unfair debt collection practices that some agencies use and how this has led to the invasion of privacy, bankruptcy, marital instability, and the loss of jobs. The reader is told what he can do about the problem.

(trade paper) ISBN 0914984322 **$9.95**

The Quick Job Hunt Guide —Robert D. Siedle

Gives techniques to use when looking for a job. Networking, Following the Ten-Day Plan, and Avoiding the Personnel Department, are some of the ways to "land that job!"

(trade paper) ISBN 0914984330 **$7.95**

Dragon Slaying For Parents —Tom Prinz, M.S.

Subtitled: Removing The Excess Baggage So You Can Be The Parent You Want To Be. Shows how Dragons such as Codependency, Low Self-Esteem and other hidden factors interfere with effective parenting. This book by a marriage, family, and child counselor, is for all parents—to assist them with the difficult task of raising responsible and confident children in the 1990's. It is written especially for parents who believe they have "tried everything!"

(trade paper) ISBN 0914984357 **$9.95**

Books & Tapes by Starburst Publishers—cont'd.

Man And Wife For Life
—Joseph Kanzlemar, Ed.D.

A penetrating and often humorous look into real life situations of married people. Helps the reader get a new understanding of the problems and relationships within marriage.

(trade paper) ISBN 0914984233 **$7.95**

Off The Floor. . . and Into Your Soup?
—Charles Christmas, Jr.

A shocking account of what goes on behind the scenes at many restaurants—high class or not. Author looks at the restaurant itself, its employees, and the food that is served to the customer. He also reveals the practical jokes, and more, that kitchen employees do to each other, and the not-so-kind things they do to patrons.

(trade paper) ISBN 0914984381 **$7.95**

Allergy Cooking With Ease
—Nicolette N. Dumke

A book designed to provide a wide variety of recipes to meet many different types of dietary and social needs, and, whenever possible, save you time in food preparation. Includes: Recipes for those special foods that most food allergy patients think they will never eat again; Timesaving tricks; and Allergen Avoidance Index.

(trade paper-opens flat) ISBN 091498442X **$12.95**

Inch by Inch . . . Is It a Cinch?
—Phyllis Miller

Is it a cinch to lose weight? If your answer is "NO," you must read this book. Read about the intimate details of one woman's struggle for love and acceptance.

(trade paper) ISBN 0914984152 **$8.95**

Alzheimer's—Does "The System" Care?
—Ted Valenti, M.S.W. & Paula Valenti, R.N.

Experts consider Alzheimer's disease to be the "the disease of the century." More than half the one million elderly people residing in American nursing homes have "senile dementia." This book reveals a unique observation as to the cause of Alzheimers's and the care of its victims.

(hard cover) ISBN 0914984179 **$14.95**

A Candle In Darkness (novel)
—June Livesay

A heartwarming novel (based on fact), set in the mountains of Ecuador. This book is filled with love, suspense, and intrigue. The first in a series of books by June Livesay.

(trade paper) ISBN 0914984225 **$8.95**

Purchasing Information

Listed books are available from your favorite Bookstore, either from current stock or special order. You may also order direct from STARBURST PUBLISHERS. When ordering enclose full payment plus $2.00* for shipping and handling ($2.50* if Canada or Overseas). Payment in US Funds only. Please allow two to three weeks minimum (longer overseas) for delivery. Make checks payable to and mail to STARBURST PUBLISHERS, P.O. Box 4123, LANCASTER, PA 17604. **Prices subject to change without notice**. Catalog available upon request.

* We reserve the right to ship your order the least expensive way. If you desire first class (domestic) or air shipment (overseas) please enclose shipping funds as follows: First Class within the USA enclose $4.00, Airmail Canada enclose $5.00, and Overseas enclose 30% (minimum $5.00) of total order. All remittance must be in US Funds.   03-92